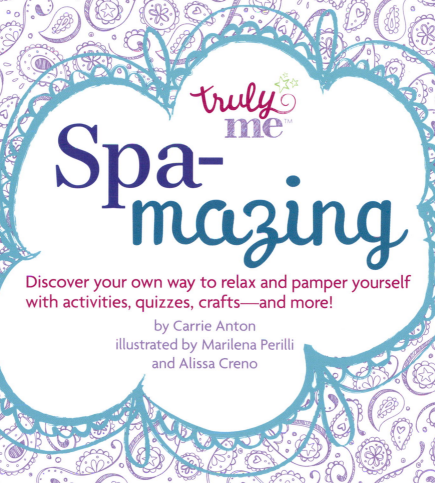

truly me™

Spa-mazing

Discover your own way to relax and pamper yourself
with activities, quizzes, crafts—and more!

by Carrie Anton
illustrated by Marilena Perilli
and Alissa Creno

Published by American Girl Publishing

16 17 18 19 20 21 LEO 10 9 8 7 6 5 4 3 2 1

Editorial Development: Carrie Anton, Emily Osborn
Art Direction and Design: Jinger Schroeder, Nancy Warneke, Lisa Wilber
Production: Jeannette Bailey, Laura Markowitz, Cynthia Stiles, Kristi Tabrizi
Photography: Chris Hynes, Mark Gillespie
Craft Stylist: Carrie Anton
Set Stylists: Ginger Lukas, Derek Brabender, Emily Osborn
Hair Stylist: Lynée Ruiz
Doll Stylist: Jane Amini
Illustrations: Marilena Perilli, Alissa Creno

Stock Photography: page 5 (girl) © iStock.com/Aleksander Kaczmarek; page 39 (koala) © iStock.com/KristianBell; page 40 (kitten) © iStock.com/Carosch; page 49 (cucumber slice) © iStock.com/Sommail

Even though instructions have been tested and results from testing were incorporated into this book, all recommendations and suggestions are made without any guarantees on the part of American Girl. Because of differing tools, materials, ingredients, conditions, and individual skills, the publisher disclaims liability for any injuries, losses, or other damages that may result from using the information in this book. Not all craft materials are tested to the same standards as toy products.

Dear Reader,

It's not easy to be true to yourself when you're stressed out and feeling like you're giving a piggyback ride to the whole world. When you're tired after a long day of school and hobbies, when you and your best friend have an argument, or when your homework seems too hard to handle, you don't feel like you. Maybe you're cranky, tired, annoyed, or sad . . . whatever emotion has come your way, it's time to unwind.

This book is full of everyday ways for you to relax, re-energize, and have fun getting your mind, body, and spirit back in balance. We've filled the pages of this book with activities, crafts, tips, treatments, and tear-outs to make pampering yourself a top priority . . . and easy, too! Take a deep breath in and out; then turn the page for some spa-mazing secrets!

Your friends at American Girl

When you see this symbol 🖐, it means you need an adult to help you with all or part of the task. ALWAYS ask for help before continuing. Ask an adult to approve all craft supplies before you use them—some are not safe for kids. When creating doll crafts, remember that dyes from supplies may bleed onto your doll or her clothes and leave permanent stains. Use lighter colors when possible, and check your doll often to make sure the colors aren't transferring to her body, her vinyl, or her clothes. And never get your doll wet! Water and heat increase dye rub-off.

Take time to do what makes your soul happy.

Stress Less Test

When you need a break, what's the best way for you to chillax?

Feeling fried? Take this quiz to find the chill-out style that is just right for you to relax.

1. What is your favorite way to study for a test?

a. with headphones on

b. pacing around my house

c. using doodled flash cards I made

d. tutoring someone else

e. hosting a slumber study party

2. Where is your favorite place at school?

a. the music room

b. the gym

c. the art room

d. my classroom

e. the playground

3. You can't sleep. What's keeping you awake?

a. I'm thinking too much about tomorrow's busy day.

b. I just can't seem to lie still.

c. I don't know what to wear to school tomorrow—I'm bored with my style.

d. My friend was crying on the bus; I hope she's OK.

e. I miss my sister. We've been too busy to just hang out together.

4. Which extracurricular activity sounds most like something you'd join?

a. Wait, just one?

b. soccer

c. craft club

d. volunteering at the library

e. student council

5. What is your most prized possession?

a. My tablet; I can listen to music, play games, do homework, and keep track of my to-do list.

b. My lucky socks; I haven't washed them since scoring the winning point.

c. My winter hat; my first no-mistakes knitting project.

d. A thank-you note; my dad gave it to me after I cleaned his car.

e. My scrapbook; it has all my favorite friend and family memories.

6. If you were to get in trouble in class, it would probably be for …

a. working on homework for another class.

b. fidgeting.

c. doodling in my notebook instead of listening.

d. hinting an answer to a friend who looks stuck.

e. passing a note to my BFF.

7. What do you dislike most about summer?

a. being bored

b. being stuck inside on rainy days

c. not being able to sell the bracelets I make to other kids at school

d. not having a study buddy

e. not seeing my friends every day

Be Still

If you answered **mostly a's,** remember to take a break from your busy schedule. Running from one activity to the next and listening to music all the time can be a bit chaotic. Your brain needs quiet time so that it can have a chance to recharge. While you may feel like you do your best when you're always on the go, don't forget to slow down and enjoy some silence, too. Take a few minutes (or longer!) and do some meditation activities, such as quietly reading a book, lying on the lawn and watching the clouds go by, or cuddling with your cat as you sit in your favorite chair. These are good activities to do every day, and also when you're feeling a little overwhelmed.

Be Active

If you answered **mostly b's,** exercise is the best way for you to chill out. While some people need quiet meditation time to recharge, you'll get the same effect by moving your body. When your mood needs a boost, taking your dog for a walk, jumping rope in your driveway, or going for a run with your older brother can do the trick. Physical activity not only helps make your body healthier and stronger, but also helps you sleep better at night and rev up your self-confidence. Get at least one hour of exercise every day in general, but use this as your go-to activity when you're feeling stressed.

Be Creative

If you answered **mostly c's,** burn some creative energy when your day isn't going your way! For crafty, DIY people, stress can often be about simply feeling uninspired. Although going to school, doing your homework, and completing your chores are all part of life, don't let boredom make them a burden. Find ways to add your own unique style to every task you do so that the more unique you make them, the more fun they feel. After all, it's hard to be stressed out when you're having a good time!

Be #1

If you answered **mostly d's,** it's time to show yourself some love. You're awesome when it comes to lending a helping hand to everyone in need, but you might be forgetting about the person who matters most—you! Helping those around you deserves a standing ovation, but sometimes it means carrying other people's problems around as your own. It doesn't mean you can't still be there for those in need, but first you need to make sure you're at your best. Spend some time pampering yourself by taking a bubble bath, practicing a new way to braid your hair, or treating yourself to a special snack. When you're stuck for an idea on being kind to yourself, just imagine what you'd do for someone else.

Be Together

If you answered **mostly e's,** call on your friends and family to keep you company. Feeling overwhelmed might be more about being lonely. Sure, you may have time with classmates at school or with your parents at dinner, but if tests, games, or other tasks are weighing on your mind, quality time with loved ones could be just the cure. To feel calm and relaxed, spend time with those closest to you. Watch a movie together, go for a nature hike, or throw a "just because" party filled with love and laughter. Skip being solo; hang with your friends and family to feel better.

Perfectly Pampered Party

SPAAHH

Gather a group of four and relax together with spa essentials and more!

Throw a spa-mazing party filled with crafts, games, treats, decor, and more that will help you and your friends relax in style.

Thank You!

11

Decor

Bath Pouf Garland: Turn bath poufs into a colorful garland to hang at your spa party. Using a plastic needle, string yarn through the center of each pouf. Tie knots on each side to keep the pouf from slipping, or string lots of poufs together to completely hide the yarn. Hang garlands with poufs in different colors, or add letters that say "Spaahh!"

Floating Bubbles: Create a bath-like feel by turning your party space into a bubbly wonderland. Hang clear plastic ornaments in different sizes (available at craft stores) from the ceiling using clear cord at varying lengths. Attach the cord using removable wall putty or clear removable tape.

Favors

Little Ladies: Turn spa tools into darling favors for friends. Attach the punch-out spa heads from the back of the book to two emery boards using adhesive dots. Wrap around two cosmetic wipes and use a ribbon to tie them closed. Attach a punch-out thank-you flag to a mini plastic cuticle pusher, and slip beneath the cosmetic wipes.

Tresses Train: Sit in a single-file line with each girl's hair tools and accessories within reach. (It's best not to share combs and brushes. And always be careful when using certain tools in different hair types. A brush that works best on straight hair can get stuck in a head full of curls. Last, never use scissors! A parent should help you decide what is best for this game.) When the clock starts, do the hair of the person sitting in front of you, with the first person doing a doll's hair. After one minute, trade places, picking up where the first "stylist" left off. Repeat one-minute rounds until everyone has worked on each other's hair.

DIY Lip Gloss: Send each of your guests home with lip gloss she makes. Make lip gloss by stirring 2 tablespoons of coconut oil that an adult has warmed in the microwave for 30 seconds until it's smooth like glue. Sprinkle in a teaspoon of fruit punch powder mix and add 2–3 drops of water. Mix together, adding more powder until the color is to your liking. Spoon or pour the mixtures into small plastic makeup jars (available at craft stores), and add the punch-out labels to the jar tops. Place in the fridge until the lip gloss hardens a bit and store in a cool place.

Fizzy Bath Bombs: Swap the bubbles for some fizzy fun. To make 4 or 5 bombs, mix together 1 cup each cornstarch, baking soda, and citric acid powder with ¼ cup Epsom salts. Separately mix 1 teaspoon vegetable oil, a few drops of food coloring, a few drops of a fragrant essential oil, and ¼ cup water. While whisking the dry ingredients, add one tablespoon of wet ingredients at a time until fully mixed— about 5 tablespoons (it should feel like wet sand). Put the mixture into each side of clear plastic ornaments so that it's slightly overflowing. Close the two sides together and let dry for 2 hours. Twist the bombs free from the mold before using in the tub.

Nail Polish Cupcake Toppers:
Add a colorful top coat to cupcakes with edible bottles of nail polish. Lightly spray a marshmallow with water and roll it in colored sugar. With help from a parent, stick half a toothpick into a 1-inch piece of licorice and place the other half into the top of the marshmallow. Top a cupcake with your custom "nail color."

Pretty Parfaits: Layer vanilla yogurt, granola, and fresh fruit in clear serving glasses or plastic cups for a pretty treat that's healthy to eat.

16

Flavored Waters: Skip the sugary pops and juices. Instead, serve naturally flavored water that's a tasty treat and good for you, too. Place the following ingredients in pitchers, pile on ice cubes, and fill with cold water. Close and store in the fridge up to 12 hours before serving.

• **Strawberry Tart:** Squeeze in quarter-cut wedges of two limes and top with 8 ounces of slightly thawed frozen strawberries. Mash the strawberries lightly with a wooden spoon.

• **Cool as a Cuke:** Fill ⅓ of the way with sliced cucumbers.

• **Citrus Sensation:** Fill ⅓ of the way with sliced oranges and lemons.

• **Berry Refreshing:** Add a sprig or two of fresh mint leaves and use a wooden spoon to twist and push on the leaves to release the flavor (just bruise them, don't tear them apart). Top with 8 ounces of slightly thawed frozen raspberries. Mash the berries lightly with a wooden spoon.

Moody Cootie Catcher

Try to feel better with these activities.

Punch out the Moody Cootie Catcher in the back of the book to see which activities will help you feel your best.

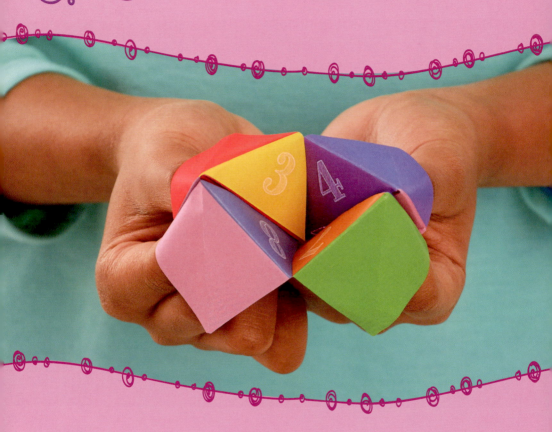

To Play:

1. Pick a color from one of the four corners.

2. Spell the color, pinching and pushing the sections apart for each letter.

3. Select a number, pinching and pushing the sections apart as you count.

4. Select one more number. Lift the flap and read the activity under that number.

Make a Mini Moody

Punch out the doll-size cootie catcher for activities that will make her day brighter.

19

Face It

Show your skin some love with a spa-style facial.

✋⭐ Mix up one of these magical masks and then follow the tips for a super four-step facial. *Note: Check with a parent and test on your inner forearm before applying to your face.*

Mix-Up Masks

 **Mediterranean Mask:** For soft, smooth skin, combine ⅓ cup olive oil with one small mashed avocado. Mix until smooth and apply to face.

 **Jack-O-Lantern Mask:** For healthier, more radiant skin, mix together ¼ cup canned plain pumpkin purée and 1 tablespoon honey.

 **Pretty Parfait Mask:** If your skin's been a bit rough lately, mix together ⅓ cup plain oatmeal, ⅓ cup warm water, 1 teaspoon honey, and 2 tablespoons of plain yogurt.

 **Fall Favorite Mask:** Combine ¼ cup natural applesauce with two tablespoons wheat germ for a mask to soothe your skin.

Want to make them all to use with your friends? Use the labels in the back of the book to help you remember which one is which.

Four-Step Facial

1.  **Get Ready:** Change into your robe and pull your hair back gently with a head-band or ponytail holder. Fill a bowl with warm water and another bowl with ice water. Find two clean washcloths and wrap a towel around your neck. Ask a parent to help you slice half a cucumber.

2. **Cleanse and Exfoliate:** Press a warm, wet wash-cloth against your face for about a minute to heat and moisten your skin. Then apply a gentle cleanser or scrub, rubbing your finger-tips in small circles to cleanse your skin. Rinse.

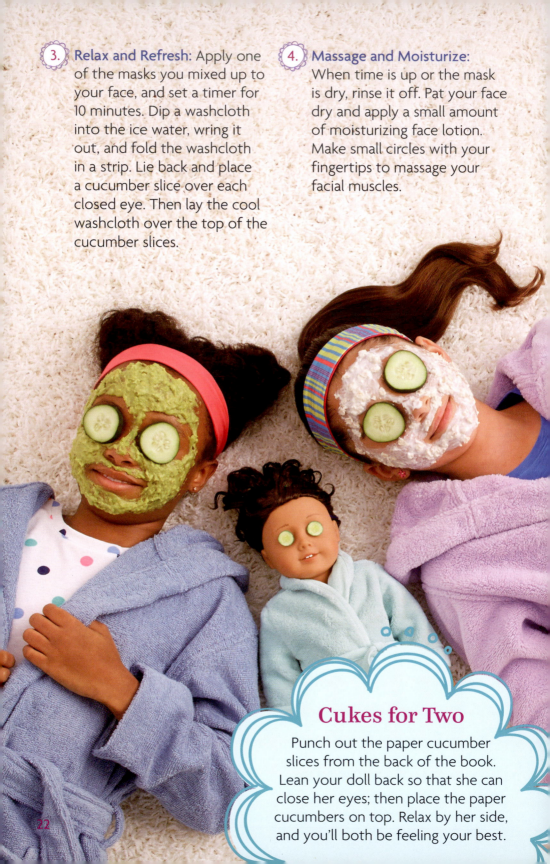

3. **Relax and Refresh:** Apply one of the masks you mixed up to your face, and set a timer for 10 minutes. Dip a washcloth into the ice water, wring it out, and fold the washcloth in a strip. Lie back and place a cucumber slice over each closed eye. Then lay the cool washcloth over the top of the cucumber slices.

4. **Massage and Moisturize:** When time is up or the mask is dry, rinse it off. Pat your face dry and apply a small amount of moisturizing face lotion. Make small circles with your fingertips to massage your facial muscles.

Cukes for Two

Punch out the paper cucumber slices from the back of the book. Lean your doll back so that she can close her eyes; then place the paper cucumbers on top. Relax by her side, and you'll both be feeling your best.

Cloudy Doodle Daydream

Look to the sky to see what the clouds say is in store for you.

Sometimes when you see objects, faces, or words take shape in a sky full of clouds, it has a lot to say about what you're thinking or how you're feeling. Use the illustrated sky space below to see what doodled clouds have to say about your mood. Draw in as few or as many clouds as you like, in any shape, any place, and in any way. Then turn the page to reveal what feelings are in your forecast.

Amount

1–3: If your sky had very few clouds, sunny days are ahead. You're feeling happy and positive. Your cares seem to drift away as easily as clouds float by.

4–6: There are a few worries on the horizon, but nothing you can't handle. Clouds always pass, and so will any matter that's troubling you.

7 or more: Things may seem serious now, but just remember this quote by Paul F. Davis: "The sun always shines above the clouds." Brighter days will return.

Shape

If your clouds look more like **animals,** you like to surround yourself with unconditional love. You don't need to prove yourself to anyone; you're great just the way you are.

If your clouds simply look like **clouds,** you appreciate the simpler things in life. You know that having lots of stuff won't make you happier. You love things for what they are just because you find them interesting.

If your clouds look more like **faces,** you might be worried about what other people think. Just remember that even though people may be looking at you, it might be simply because they like what they see.

If your clouds look more like **letters,** you tend to feel things deeply. Don't hold in your emotions; share with a sibling or a friend, write them in your journal, or paint a picture of how you feel.

Location

High in the sky: If most of your doodled clouds are so high in the sky that they are practically floating off the page, then you're feeling full of cheer. There's a bounce in your step because today was especially great . . . then again, every day is that way!

Hanging low: If the clouds you drew were of things you love, then you hold them near and dear to your heart. However, if the clouds represented things that are weighing on your mind, then the closer they are to you, the more stressful they may seem. Take a moment to relax, and soon the clouds won't seem quite so gloomy.

Here and there: Life is full of ups and downs, and no one accepts that better than you. If you're feeling down one day, you know that an "up" is just around the corner.

Om on the Go

No matter where you go, take your yoga with you.

Getting Started

When doing yoga, remember to:

- find a quiet spot.
- wear loose clothes.
- use a sticky yoga mat for cushioning.
- go barefoot so that you won't slip.
- practice on an empty stomach (wait an hour if you've eaten a meal).
- move in slow, controlled motions.
- breathe deeply.

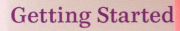

Salute the Sun

Give your morning a great start by greeting the day and energizing your body with the first few poses of a Sun Salutation.

1. Stand with your feet hip-width apart and your palms together at your chest (as if you're praying).

2. As you breathe in, sweep your arms out to the sides and overhead, while looking up.

3. As you breathe out, bend over and try to touch your toes, bending your knees as much as needed.

4. Breathe in and bring your body up slowly with your arms out to the sides. Bring your arms overhead again and look up. Breathe out as you slowly lower your hands back to your chest with palms together.

5. Repeat several times.

You can do these poses again anytime you need to wake up your body and your mind.

Practice Poses While it's best to learn yoga from someone who has experience, there are a few poses that are great for beginners. Punch out the yoga cards in the back of the book. The fronts show what the poses look like, and the backs explain tips for best technique. Take the travel cards with you so that you can practice wherever you go.

Downward-Facing Doll

Give your doll her own mat to practice her poses. Cut out a piece of craft foam or felt (both available at craft stores) so that it is 19 inches long by 9 inches wide. When it comes time to store the mat, roll it up and tie each end with 8-inch pieces of decorative ribbon.

Snacks for the Soul

Food to help improve your mood.

Feeling good happens from the inside out—that's why they say *you are what you eat*. Try these six easy, healthy, and tasty go-to snacks when you need food to fuel your mood.

Cucumber Crunch Sandwiches: Feeling blah? Get a boost with refreshing cucumber mini snacks. Ask an adult to carefully cut up a cucumber into about ½-inch thick slices. Place a small slice of cheese on top of the cucumber slice. Add a folded slice of lunch meat and then top with a small swirl of mustard. Add another cucumber slice to close the "sandwich."

Banana Bites: Using a microwave-safe container, melt about 1 cup of dark chocolate chips in the microwave on medium heat for 30 seconds. Remove and stir. If not melted, repeat heating and stirring to avoid burning. Once melted, slip a banana chunk onto a colorful straw and dip it in the chocolate. Quickly dip the banana bit into another bowl of your favorite topping, such as sprinkles, shredded coconut, granola, or crushed almonds. Place the banana bites in the freezer to cool.

 Cereal Sticks: Take your cereal on the go with these no-bake bars. Put ¼ cup honey, ¼ cup brown sugar, and 2 tablespoons butter in a microwave-safe bowl and heat on medium heat for one minute, or until melted. Stir the melted ingredients together until kind of foamy. Add two teaspoons of vanilla extract and stir again. Mix in one cup of cereal and one cup combination of craisins, raisins, or nuts. Use a spatula to flatten the mixture on a wax-paper-covered cookie sheet. Place in the fridge overnight, and ask an adult to cut into bars when ready to eat. Store in the fridge.

Yogurt Brr-Berries: Chill out with this snack that is as cool as it is tasty. Place a blueberry (or whatever berry you like best!) on a toothpick. Dunk it in a bowl of vanilla-flavored Greek yogurt and swirl it around until the entire berry is covered. Drop the berry onto a wax-paper-covered cookie sheet. Repeat until all your berries are dipped, or until your cookie sheet is filled. Place the sheet in the freezer and let harden. When done, enjoy your cold and creamy treat!

Apple Duper Dippers: Turn an off day into a slam dunk with this perfect apple snack. Apple slices are great all on their own, but for more fun flavor, give them a dip. Mix together ⅓ cup honey-flavored Greek yogurt with 1 tablespoon creamy peanut butter, 1 tablespoon honey, and ⅓ teaspoon cinnamon. Once it's all stirred up, dunk in your apple chunks.

Crepe-sadillas: When cranky ways just won't quit, feed your hunger with this yummy snack that is good for breakfast, lunch, or an after-school bite. Spread peanut butter on a whole wheat tortilla. Place sliced strawberries on one half and then add a few dark chocolate chips on top. Fold the tortilla in half and use a pizza cutter to slice into easy-to-grab wedges.

Nailed It!

Try our tricks for nails that are nice and neat.

Want to give your fingers a pop of color (and your parents are cool with you painting your nails), but think you don't have the steady hands to make it happen? Think again. Lay down paper on your work area and then follow these tips for some high-five manicure makeovers!

Ten Tips for Perfect Polish

1. Roll the bottle of nail polish between your palms to mix well.

2. Apply the first brushstroke in the middle of the nail.

3. Apply polish in thin coats.

4. Paint one hand at a time, and let it dry before starting the other hand.

5. Team up with a friend to paint each other's nails.

6. Use a kid-friendly nail polish in a quick-dry formula.

7. If you get polish on the skin around your nails, let it dry and then rub it off with a cotton swab dipped in nail polish remover.

8. When applying a second coat, don't press down too hard on the first layer.

9. Blowing on your nails to dry them will dull their shine.

10. Prevent goopy polish by storing bottles in the refrigerator (if your parent says it's okay).

Just Add Art

Here are seven ways you can turn your mani into its own masterpiece.

1. **Rainbow Bright:** Instead of just one color for all ten nails, give each nail a color of its own. Not sure which color to use? Punch out and assemble the "Spin the Nail Polish" spinner from the back of the book. Place a different bottle on each pie wedge. Spin to see which color to use. It's also a fun game to play at a sleepover.

2. **DIY Dots:** Give your nails polka dots using one rounded end of a bobby pin or rounded toothpick. Pour a little nail polish on a grease-resistant paper plate, and lightly dip in the bobby pin. Add one or more dots in a design.

3. **Punch Out:** Use a small decorative paper punch on a piece of removable tape. On clean or dry painted nails, place the stencil over your nail and lightly paint over it. Carefully remove the tape before it dries to prevent peeling. Let dry. Add to one nail, or let all your fingers in on the fun.

4. **Jagged Edge:** Cut a piece of removable tape with decorative-edged scissors. On clean or dry painted nails, place the tape edge on your nail and lightly paint over it. Carefully remove the tape before it dries to prevent peeling. Let dry.

5. **Sparkle and Shine:** Before your nail polish dries, when it's just a little tacky, use an old makeup brush or small clean paintbrush to dust on loose, sparkly eye shadow. Once dry, add a clear coat over the top to make the shimmer last.

6. **Marker Magic:** Create free-hand nail art using a nontoxic metallic fine-tip permanent marker. Draw onto nails already painted and dry, and if you make a mistake, use rubbing alcohol on a cotton swab to wipe clean and start over.

Mini Manicure

Your doll can have nice nails, too. Tear off tiny pieces of washi tape to put on her nails, or use small paper punches to create a fun shape to stick on. Peel off when done.

7. **Sticky Stuff:** For a more temporary look that you can change each day, add strips or punch-outs of washi tape (also known as paper tape, available at craft stores) to your painted nails. The tape comes in all kinds of colors and patterns, so you can even match your outfits each day.

Sleep Style

Bedtime crafts for sweet dreams.

Sleep helps your body recover from one day and gear up for the next. Try to keep the same bedtime every night—even on the weekends! Before you settle in, do a number of things in the same order, such as brushing your teeth, setting out your clothes for the next day, and snuggling in bed with a good book. If you're not big on heading to bed or just have trouble sleeping sometimes, make these crafts to help get you snoozing.

ZZZs Journal

If worries are keeping you awake or you have a lot of ideas you've been thinking about, put them on paper to stop them from racing around your head. Make a mini journal to keep by your bedside with a pen or pencil. Whenever something is bothering you while you're in bed, write it down so you can fall back to sleep quickly.

To make: Use the template in the back of the book. Trace the outside edges of the rectangle shape and mark the holes on one piece of two-sided scrapbook paper and about 3 sheets of plain white paper. Cut out each sheet and use a hole-punch where you marked the holes. Fold each sheet in half across the punched holes. Stack the paper so that the scrapbook paper is on the outside. String baker's twine through the holes and tie with a bow. Decorate the front of your journal with the punch-outs from the back of the book.

Pillow Pal

If you sometimes feel fearful being alone in your room at night, have a buddy by your side to keep you company.

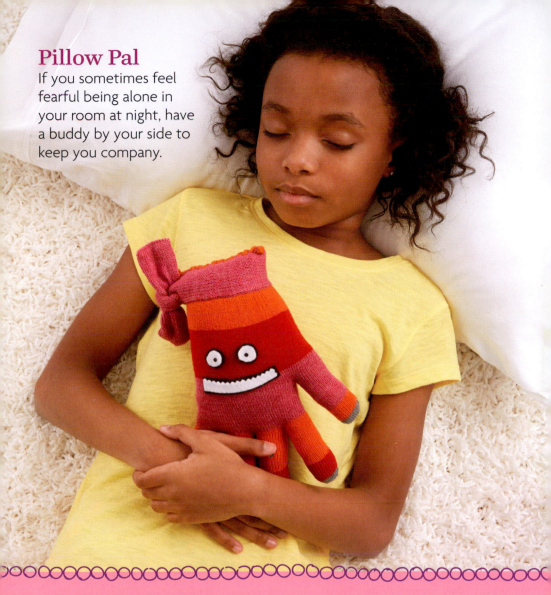

To make: Stuff an old knit glove with batting (found at craft stores), making sure to fill each finger. Fold an 18-inch piece of yarn in half and thread both ends through the eye of a plastic needle. Hold the glove opening shut and, starting from one end, sew through both sides, making sure not to pull the folded yarn end through. String the needle through the loop and pull taut.

Sew along the edge of the glove opening, always inserting from one side and pulling through to the opposite side. When you reach the other end, remove the needle and tie a knot. Trim off the excess yarn. Give your pillow pal a silly face using felt pieces and craft glue. When dry, tuck your pal into bed with you and say goodnight.

Don't Disturb Door Hanger

If your house tends to get noisy at nighttime, let others know you're trying to sleep with a helpful door hanger.

To make: Punch out the door hanger in the back of the book. Color it in and decorate it with embellishments. Before you head to bed, hang it on your door, so that others know to keep the noise down.

Sleep Sack

The scent of lavender is said to have a calming effect, which is perfect for soothing you to sleep. Lay this scent-filled pillow over your eyes to help you drift off to dreamland.

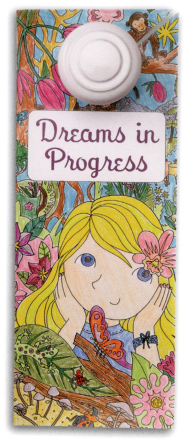

To make: In a tall cup, mix 1 cup of uncooked rice with 2 tablespoons of dried lavender (found at health-food stores). Stretch the end of a clean, soft sock over the mouth of the cup. Turn the cup upside down to fill the sock with the rice mixture. Knot the end of the sock, or secure it with a rubber band or tied ribbon. Lie back and place the pillow over your eyes. Breathe in the soft scent and relax.

Lighten Up

While darkness is supposed to help cue the brain that it's time for sleep, sometimes a room that's too dark can cause you to worry. Add a soft glow to your space by creating a night-light that will shine the way to slumber land.

To make: Stick adhesive-backed rhinestones (available at craft stores) to a jar. Cover the entire body of the jar, leaving the bottom flat. Drop in a battery-operated tea light to add a bit of brightness to a too-dark room.

Just
Chilling

Sweet Dream Sticks

Create a mobile using colorful sticks to send you softly to sleep.

To make: Find 3–5 sticks from outside. Clean, dry, and paint them in different patterns using acrylic paints. When dry, find the center point of the bottom stick and wrap baker's twine around it. Tie a knot but don't cut the strings. Tie another knot in the string about 1 inch up, so that the next stick can rest on it. Repeat these steps with all the sticks. Tie the sticks to the inside ring of a 4-inch embroidery hoop. Tie another string at the top, from which it can hang. Punch out one of the dream catcher patterns from the back of the book and attach it with a glue stick. Hang it in your room for sweet dreams.

How was your spa-mazing day?

Send your letters to

Truly Me: Spa-mazing! Editor
American Girl
8400 Fairway Place
Middleton, WI 53562

(Sorry, but photos can't be returned. All comments
and suggestions received by American Girl may be
used without compensation or acknowledgment.)

Here are some other American Girl books you might like:

Each sold separately. Find more books online at americangirl.com.

Thank You!

Thank You!

Thank You!

Thank You!

Create a happiness collage from magazine pictures.

Take eight deep belly breaths.

Smell a scent that makes you smile.

Put on some music and dance.

Write a poem in less than one minute.

Pet a furry creature—even a stuffed animal.

Compliment a friend or family member.

Write in your journal.

To Fold:

1. Flip the Moody Cootie Catcher facedown and fold the four corners along the solid lines.

2. Flip over so that the folds are now facedown. Fold the four corners along the dotted lines.

3. Fold the entire square in half and reopen it. Repeat folding in half in the other direction.

4. Using two hands, slip thumbs and first fingers into the openings. Pinch and push the sections apart.

Style your doll's hair.

Give your doll a hug.

Make a bracelet for your doll.

Sing a song together.

Tell your doll a joke.

Pretend you're on a safari together.

Do a silly dance together.

Draw a picture of your doll.

Cat Pose

When you practice this posture, imagine a cat stretching after a nap.

1. Start on your hands and knees with your hands under your shoulders and your knees under your hips. Palms should be flat on the floor and your toes should be pointing backward.

2. Breathe in. When you exhale, round your back upward with your head dropping down and your tailbone tucked in. Pull your belly in toward your spine.

3. Pause for a moment or two in this position.

4. Repeat steps 2 and 3 five times smoothly, so that your movement follows your breath.

Butterfly Pose

Picture yourself calm and free, like a butterfly.

1. Sit on the floor with your back straight and shoulders relaxed.

2. Place the soles of your feet together in front of you.

3. Hold your feet with your hands and gently pull your feet in toward you so that you feel a gentle stretch in your inner legs.

4. Breathe deeply several times, gazing at a point of focus or with closed eyes.

Cat Pose

When you practice this posture, imagine a cat stretching after a nap.

1. Start on your hands and knees with your hands under your shoulders and your knees under your hips. Palms should be flat on the floor and your toes should be pointing backward.

2. Breathe in. When you exhale, round your back upward with your head dropping down and your tailbone tucked in. Pull your belly in toward your spine.

3. Pause for a moment or two in this position.

4. Repeat steps 2 and 3 five times smoothly, so that your movement follows your breath.

Butterfly Pose

Picture yourself calm and free, like a butterfly.

1. Sit on the floor with your back straight and shoulders relaxed.

2. Place the soles of your feet together in front of you.

3. Hold your feet with your hands and gently pull your feet in toward you so that you feel a gentle stretch in your inner legs.

4. Breathe deeply several times, gazing at a point of focus or with closed eyes.